Empathic Indulgence

Jeremy Mckemy

BookLeaf Publishing

India | USA | UK

Presentation by *BookLeaf Publishing*

Web: www.bookleafpub.com

E-mail: info@bookleafpub.com

ISBN: 9789360946142

First edition 2024

This book is dedicated to Larry Quinn. He was a father and an accomplished writer and musician. Through his efforts, his vision of an interactive art garden is coming to life. Years of dedicated work has been completed by Larry and other veterans to bring joy to our prized aging veteran community. He was awe inspiring individual who was larger than life.

ACKNOWLEDGEMENT

I wanna thank my family and friends for always believing in me and being there and cheering me on in my life.

Ode to Larry

Bright colors suit his soul,
Shining up outta that hole,
Bring forth a common goal,
Bring peace and harmony to a war torn heart,
Bring solitude from within to start,
Art for healing is what this is,
Larry's vision,
He was a whizz,
He cares about veterans health,
All their struggles he knew well,
Knowing the moral dilemma,
The feelings of going to hell,
How do we get in,
How do we unring that bell,
But the art makes us create,
Makes us think and contemplate,
Knowing it's healing us make it so much better,
If it's a water color,
Or knitting a sweater,
So move on with his vision and know,
He is smiling down,
Watching all of it,
With feelings of Van Gogh!!

Miss Mousy Mom

Thank you for always being there,
Always had my back,
Like a sturdy chair,
Holding my imperfections,
Teaching me life lessons,
Always so positive and joyful,
So much power in your words,
Every sentence soulful,
Good with God,
Not scared of death,
But I pray God doesn't test me,
With your end yet,
I'm not ready to lose you,
Honestly, I never will be,
The amount of love I have for you,
Yes, it's immeasurable,
It's been amazing with a heart full,
So much nurturing,
Patience to no end,
All the love in the world,
Your way I'm gonna send!!

Haas as a Rock

To my brother who has been my rock,
You have had a positive influence on me,
Holding me steady,
Like the roots of a tree,
There's nothing I wouldn't do for you,
Live in heaven,
Or fight like hell,
To make sure you're alright in this life,
You picked me up when I fell,
I'll never forget that,
It meant so much,
A love I needed,
In your brotherly touch,
You're my hero and that's a fact,
Tougher than a two dollar steak,
Strong as a silverback,
So I'll be here if you need to call on me,
You name the place and time,
I'll be there with gusto,
I might not be in my prime,
But I'll fight till my end for you,
I just want you to know that,
You know it's true,
Though I hope you already knew that,
And you already do.

Proud Beyond Measure

Here is a ode to my son,
He's a light that'll never be extinguished,
So bright and distinguished,
Wise beyond his years,
Turned out amazing, squashing all my fears,
I was worried I wasn't there enough,
He took all the love I gave to him,
Though I wasn't around,
Gritted his teeth and acted tough,
Somehow he turned into the best of men,
Salt of the earth,
Thinking twice with no thought of sin,
Honest and selfless,
With a compassion to serve,
Guarding our great nation,
Way better than we deserve,
Just know that I love you completely,
With all my heart,
A love that's forever,
Never to part!

Celebrate Dr. Owczarski

Dedication to one's self,
You've stayed true,
Consistently bettering yourself,
There you go,
Just being you,
Full of knowledge and intelligent wealth,
Knowing you can make a difference,
Overflowing with kindness,
Your accomplishment is so amazing,
Such class and elegance,
So accomplished,
This graduation has great relevance,
Surmounts to a top tier title,
With a huge benevolence,
Social work has been blessed,
Social work rock star of the highest stature,
Mending people,
Suturing a lot of society's fractures,
Making all the difference,
You really matter,
I've never witnessed a person so special,
With so much potential,
Who adds so much to one's life,
So exponential,
Adoration for your craft,

As long as it's social work,
And not math,
You are deserving of the biggest celebration,
The ultimate in education,
So many years of restless nights,
All the thousands of hours of preparation,
Page after page,
So much information,
Volumes of work,
You're such a inspiration,
Not partially,
Let the world know there is a new Doctor in
house,
Dr. Owczarski!!

Call to Honor

Nothing but everything,
True love in its highest form,
Transforming lives,
Living through the storm,
Knowing your role,
Keeping up,
Being mindful,
Staying tough,
Unadulterated patriotism,
Trained and ready,
Life long mannerisms,
So much pride it beams like sun,
Boot polish and a gun,
Hurry up and wait,
Through the mist of freedom,
Proudly reciting the oath,
To protect this country,
Above self preservation,
You can't boil it down,
To a single operation,
But freedom is the inspiration,
That called us to service,
Brought on the selfless act,
Willing to die for the greater good,
Camaraderie above all else,

Brotherhood in fact,
Life long pact,
Forever instilled values,
We got each others back.

The Ranch

Hiccumups and pickup trucks,
Hound dogs and flying ducks,
So much nature,
Back yard chicken clucks,
All the things that I dream,
When I think of a brook or stream,
Ponds brimming with fish,
Flying around at night were the bats,
Setting out milk for the damn barn cats,
Sitting still plinking at the damn barn rats,
All the things I remember,
Youngster days of a forgotten September,
Feeding hogs,
Mash and corn cobs,
Electric fences,
Keep in the boar,
All the hawks up, up, and soar,
Chased by the geese,
Running for my life,
Not caring in the least,
Outside till night,
Growing up on the ranch,
Best childhood ever,
Forked branch,
Sling shots and never miss, never,

Theses were the times,
That shaped my life,
Dreams so thick you can cut them with a knife.

Summertime in Mendo

Green trees,
Yes, please,
Many thanks,
Riverbanks,
All the woods,
Always understood,
Where to live,
Where I could,
But I'll ways go back to visit,
The land of greenery,
So much time,
So many memories,
Hot cocoa and campfires,
Fishing line and needle nose pliers,
All the time spent in those trees,
Make me pray and hit my knees,
Thankful for all the smoke,
That saturated my clothes,
Water from the damn garden hose,
Friends and cousins playing around,
Riding bikes,
Until that whistle sounds,
Then dinner time,
Happy to eat,
Burn your plate,

Then it's back to the street,
Summertime in Mendo,
Like a big crescendo,
Then it's back to school,
Break is over.

Tears Perfect Purpose

They cleanse us,
Of those feelings of grief,
Let it out,
Release,
Let them flow,
It's ok to cry,
It's impossible to understand,
Or sometimes a reason why,
How it works so well,
Soothes the soul,
Resets our chi,
Brings us to center,
Roots from a tree,
It's about realizing it's not draining us,
It's giving back all the wishes wished,
Words not said,
Kisses not kissed,
Life's moments missed,
Just know tears are powerful and pure,
They bring us up to endure,
Then let them out randomly,
Maybe a birth or a death,
To never cry is insanity,
Let it out,
Take a deep breath,

Angels fuel,
Tears are emotion embodied,
They are real,
Not photocopied,
So many reasons but one answer,
Let it out and weep,
It'll overwhelm you,
Don't stow it too deep,
Bring them out and let them cascade,
Pick up the pieces,
Tears puts the pin back in the grenade!

Feelings

It's beyond description,
Past depiction,

Its feelings,

We're a slave to them,
We can try to change them,
We can but deal with them,

When they're sad,
It's a dark cloud,
Walking around dumping,
Saying negative thoughts aloud,

When you're proud,
Beaming with pride,
Banging your chest,
Along for the ride,

When your rage goes,
Makes you mad,
Boils your blood,
Do things that are bad,

Unknown toils and troubles,

Full of doubt,
Unfavorable outcomes,
Makes you shout.

When they are happy,
It's a beautiful thing,
A rush of emotion,
The heavens sing.

For Me

Feeling so defeated,
So drained and depleted,
Sucked of all my positive,
I'm here and I'm cognitive,
But my soul has been hit,
I do this to myself,
In my feelings so hard,
I bang my head on a shelf,
But I know I can conquer this,
Get back my gusto,
My light, that's my bliss,
I need to work on myself,
And that's for sure,
So much has happened, it's a blur,
I need to slow down,
Take my time to process this,
I am the only one who can make me happy,
Keep me sane,
And stay out of the negative and crappy,
I know that these feelings are bunk,
I need to lose them and put them in a trunk,
Pull myself together,
And get my self outta this funk!!

Smile

Just smile,
Keep up that shine,
Sometime we're drained,
Energy's in a bind,
But remember to keep grinning,
Keep staying positive,
Positive thoughts from the beginning,
We're only here a little while,
Fleeting seconds,
Remember to smile!!
Your inner beauty projects outward,
Sharpens steel,
Brings the good towards,
Your a big deal,
So you have a lot looking up to you,
Wondering where and the what,
Happy is what to pursue,
Recharge the banks,
Gladness ensues,
Realize how lucky we are,
To have these wonderful times,
Accept the goodness God has given us,
From the talents he's granted,
Positivity is a must,
We are all special and deserving of happiness,

Me I'm full of Zelle,
Be fabulous!

19

Love Myself

One of those days you say this is the one, The
one I've been waiting for,
I prayed so hard my knees are sore,
Wishing and thinking, "Is this the sum?"
Of all my dedication,
All years of failed and learning,
Will I finally love myself today,
Fully and completely,
Love myself discreetly,
Trust myself today,
See myself in a bright light,
See myself in a better way,
Knowing I'm trying to cope,
Washing the bad feelings,
Rinsing off the soap,
Bringing myself to love myself,
Get back myself,
Because of myself,
For myself!

Expand Your Faith in Love

I just gotta keep my faith in love,
Can't lose all the beautiful feelings,
The ones that float in your eyes,
That quirky crooked smile,
Glint in a lovers' eyes,
Curvaceous ponderance ,
I want that back in my file,
I haven't had those in a while,
I'm gonna walk that mile,
To try to achieve,
A load of those memories,
In a huge pile,
Grins from ear to ear,
Happy times,
Throughout the years,
As the world spins,
Fueled by love,
Stay humble knowing it drives us,
One way or the other,
We're all on the bus,
Next stop blissfulness,
Celebrate with cheerfulness,
So eat and be merry,
Slow down and take that ferry,
You never know who you'll meet,

When you slow down and overcome defeat,
It can be so special,
Maybe just as sweet,
As the love you lost,
The ice will melt,
From the frigid frost,
Just don't let it stagnate,
And grow moss,
Keep up taking care,
Don't forget to floss,
Pick the broken pieces out of your craw,
Accepting of every flaw,
So your heart will open again,
And accept it when it comes,
No more losers and bums,
Gotta have some standards,
Functional and heart expanders.

Prepared Heart!!

My heart is big and mighty,
I just need to clean it up - tidy,
I'm gonna be alright,
Try with all my might,
Try to stay positive and bright,
Never lose my magnificent light,
Keep up the good times,
All the fun, with a twist of limes,
I'm like a burning welding arc,
So brigh. Oh, how it shines,
Too much and you'll be blind,
So much that only blood's been able to handle it,
Without kindling it,
Someday, I'll find the one,
The one who revolves around me,
Like I'm the sun,
One that matches my glimmer,
Ready for the long haul,
Set it to simmer,
Build those flavors,
Spice of life,
I'll keep sharpening my pencil,
I'll keep sharpening my knife,
Keep up my skills,
Like a fresh pie in a window sill,

Keep paying loves' bills,
Shining like a diamond,
Faceted with so many faces,
Ready to go to heavenly places,
Match my energy and effort,
All I bring to the table,
Tired of getting hurt,
Can it happen,
Or, is it a fable?

Same Heart

The same heart that breaks during grief,
Is the same heart that warms for a belief,
Knowing the story is ever changing,
Just takes work and rearranging,
A twist here and there,
A lot of tears and banging,
Hammering of the soul,
Pounding out feelings,
The same full heart is the goal,
Chasing a high once achieved,
Built confidence that will never leave,
Put your heart out for people to see,
Heart so tender and sweet,
But strong as can be,
Just know, it's not always free,
A heavy heart can bring you to your knees!

Good Tidings

Give thanks for the day,
In a fully coherent way,
Bring forth joy and happiness,
Put all the negative aside,
Lose all the crappiness,
Rejoice in knowing each and every day is a gift,
If you live to bring smiles,
Loads of love,
In huge stacks and piles,
Stay positive in the glory of days' miracles,
From the smallest happenstance,
With the frequency in speedy intervals,
Spread the cheer!!
Knowing it's around us,
Let the love appear,
Let the love seep from our pores,
Smiling eyes,
That no one ignores,
Be so sweet and bright,
The world spins with the frequency of love,
It's the most important thing,
Whatever you believe you look above,
Bask in it,
Know it surrounds you,
It is the way of love!

Cooking

Cooking is passion,
Spice of life,
Call me old fashion,
Fork, spoon, and knife,
Season to taste,
Fresh Roma's,
Tomato paste,
Old world simplicity,
With just the right salinity,
Flavor that pops the taste buds,
From pom-fritz,
To mashed spuds,
Simple but masterfully,
Butter and all purpose,
Proteins and artistry,
A cup of creativity,
A spoon of acidity,
The right atmosphere,
Perfect humidity,
From easy-set, to using correct Maillard,
To a light color, to the heavily charred,
Cooking in all shapes and forms,
Brings forth forethought,
Brings forth carefully laid plans,
So much thought and time,

As much as hourglass sand,
A high a level of execution,
My favorite conclusion,
Without the proper dilution,
So fun creating a great meal,
Full belly, tasty solution!

Today and Tonight

Sometimes you gotta let go of the wheel,
Ride that ride,
See where it takes you,
Stride for stride,
Know that this ride is new,
For you and I,
It will creak and whine,
But a love like this is few,
Far from ordinary,
It's gotta be so hard,
Going from the pain you've endured,
I know you don't wanna let go,
When you've just gathered the raines,
Got yourself back through all of loves pains,
Just know I'm on the same ride,
So many similarities,
So much pride,
Let go!!
Just glide.
There will be turbulence, sure,
Dips and dives,
But we can pilot this vessel,
Smooth transition,
To both of us with full hearts,
There will be hard times,

That's part of life,
So let's not live in the past or future,
Let's live in today and tonight.

Deliriously Overwhelming

Bubbling,
Cup flowing over,
So many feelings,
So much love,
Like an onion,
Off with the peelings,
Way high above,
More pleasure than I've ever experienced,
Wings of a turtle dove,
Feelings so mysterious,
Highs I've never felt,
I'm damn delirious,
Feelings I've never been dealt,
Such the vision of fully stocked heart,
Softens any hardened heart I've ever had,
Opens me up,
Like a blooming flower,
Love built high,
Like Sears Tower!!

Butterflies

Butterflies,
Fluttering inside,
So many feelings,
Incoming tide,
Rushing from my heart,
Not sure what this is,
But I like it,
Filling the night air from the start,
Super blue moon on my mind,
Got me twisted,
Heart in a bind,
Thinking of no other interests,
Just you,
I'm blind,
Just singularly happy,
Floaty feelings swirling,
Ecstasy whirling,
Earthquaking,
Fresh baking,
World shaking,
Fulfilled motivation,
Full on adoration.